Hanna-Barbera's
THE GREATEST ADVENTURE
STORIES FROM THE BIBLE

# DAVID AND GOLIATH

text by
## Christine L. Benagh

*Based on a script by Harvey Bullock*

ABINGDON PRESS
*Nashville*

Two young friends, Derek and Margo, are taking part in a very important dig in the Middle East. It is the opportunity of a lifetime for them to accompany her father, an archaeologist, on this expedition.

Most days their young nomad friend Moki, who is very curious about these things, joins them to ask a hundred questions and to keep things generally lively.

One especially hot and tiring day, the three friends are digging in their assigned spot, when the sand suddenly begins to give way. "Quick sand," shouts Moki as the three

---

DAVID AND GOLIATH

ISBN 0-687-15741-2

MANUFACTURED BY THE PARTHENON PRESS AT NASHVILLE, TENNESSEE, UNITED STATES OF AMERICA

spiral down, down, down in a funnel of
sand.

Then just as unexpectedly the air is clear,
and they are in an enormous room. What a
spectacle! It is filled with treasure of every
sort—vases, jars, statues, jewelry and
ornaments, pillars, furniture of gold and
ivory.

"How magnificent," whispers Derek in
awe.

"Wow," murmurs Moki.

Margo has moved ahead of the others
toward a huge bronze door. The latch
fastening the two massive panels is a
golden scarab beetle. She puts her hand on
the scarab, translating its message: *All who
enter here go back in time.* Suddenly, the
great doors swing open into what appears
to be a cavern of light.

"Come on," she calls, and without
hesitation the others follow.

They step over the threshold and —

The flash of light blinded Margo, Derek, and Moki as they went through the opening. When they could see again there was no trace of the doorway, and they were enveloped in darkness. It was night, but they could just make out the lines of a little town ahead of them. There was a great roar, a blast of sound, and the town seemed to burst into flames. They heard shouts and screams, metal clanging and horses neighing.

"It must be a battle," Derek exclaimed.

"Let's try to see what's going on, but be on your guard."

They crawled up a sandhill and flattened themselves to watch as a terrible scene unfolded before their eyes. Soldiers were attacking the village. Children ran frightened and screaming through the streets. Now and again spears came flying through the air. Horses reared and chariots capsized, throwing the riders to the ground. All the gruesome details of the struggle were silhouetted against the glow of the fire.

"Look at that soldier!"
Margo couldn't believe her
eyes. An enormous warrior in
heavy armor towered above
the rest and was going about
his bloody work with relish.
"He must be ten feet tall."

"At least," gasped Moki.
"Wow, what if this is a land
of giants?"

"I don't want to meet him
or any other like him," said
Derek. "No one is paying any
attention to us. Let's go."

Without further discussion,
they set out. The glow from
the fire lighted their way as
they ran in the direction of a
clump of palm trees. "Let's
rest here," said Margo. "I'm
tired, and there are trees.
That means there may be
water close by. We can see in
the morning."

But morning brought a most unpleasant surprise.

"Where did all those soldiers come from?" gasped Moki, peering around his mound of sand.

"And look," Derek pointed. "There's that big guy. Let's get out of here."

They turned to run, but their way was blocked by a large man, very dark. "Halt!" he shouted. Then he herded them, not very gently, into the center of the camp. The place was full of morning bustle. Some soldiers were preparing breakfast, others were feeding the horses. In one tent they were repairing weapons, and in another they were tending the wounded, who lay moaning on every side.

"O mighty captain of the Philistines, I have three prisoners. I found them spying at the edge of the camp. It is plain they are not Hebrews, and they do not belong to our people."

"They do now," snapped the captain. "Put them to work. These two can help the chariot menders." He indicated Derek and Moki. "The female will only be good for carrying water. Set her to it." Margo was dragged away by a burly soldier.

"We're really in a mess now," whispered Derek.

"Let's run for it," said Moki.

"How can we, with Margo on the other side of the camp?"

"Get to work there," barked the sergeant. "That wheel must be reset."

"I haven't had much experience with chariots," mumbled Moki.

"Silence," roared the man, "if you value your life." He was advancing toward them when a group of soldiers came running by.

The sergeant turned and grabbed the shoulder of one. "Where are you going?"

"It's Goliath," said the soldier. "That huge fellow who joined the battle last night. He's offering a wager. He is willing to fight six men at one time, and he claims he can beat them." The sergeant released his hold, and the soldier ran after the others, with the officer close behind.

"Did you hear that? Six guys! This I gotta see." Moki took off after the soldiers.

"Yeah, let's go," said Derek. "We might run into Margo."

As they approached the tent where all the noise was coming from, they saw Margo staggering beneath the weight of the waterpails hanging from a yoke across her shoulders.

She was overjoyed to see her friends and joined them to watch this unusual wrestling match.

As they approached the cooking tent, they saw six big, husky Philistines crouched around the fire.

"This Goliath fellow must be big on brawn and small on brains," commented Derek.

At this moment Goliath himself entered. "Correct that," said Moki. "It's those gorillas who are making the mistake."

The three visitors did not go inside the tent, but flopped on the ground to peer beneath the flap.

At that moment, the six brawny cooks began to circle Goliath, ready to spring. But before a signal could be given, the giant reached out, gathered the three immediately in front of him, and banged their heads together. Then he dropped their unconscious forms to the ground. At this, two of the remaining cooks beat a hasty retreat by crawling through Goliath's huge outspread legs and running off into the desert.

"Now's our chance," said Derek.

"Our chance?" squeaked Moki. "Leave me out. I'm not fighting that giant."

"I mean our chance to escape. Everyone is looking at the fight. What are we waiting for?"

"But there's no place to hide," objected Margo. "They will see us the minute they look up."

"Not if we are inside those baskets," grinned Derek.

And so it happened that three large wicker baskets began to move mysteriously over the ground while the Philistine soldiers were watching Goliath dispatch the last luckless fellow. That poor man found himself lifted into the air above the giant's head and twirled vigorously before being heaved over the heads of the spectators.

The crowd roared, and the baskets stopped moving. Looking through the wicker Derek could see that the fight was finished.

"Then we are too," Moki sighed.

"Don't give up yet," urged Margo. "Look." A two-horse chariot was speeding toward them churning the dust as it came.

"We can disappear behind that curtain of dust," said Derek.

The three crouched as the chariot wheeled nearer. When it passed, they tossed the baskets aside and ran, ran until they literally dropped from exhaustion.

When Moki, Margo, and Derek had recovered breath and strength enough to look around, they noticed that the countryside was somewhat different. There was more vegetation, grass, and some trees scattered over rolling hills. Nearby a flock of sheep grazed.

"It would be nice to know where we are now." Margo looked about.

"I think we are in some place where they worship lions. Look at that statue over there." Moki pointed to the top of a nearby hill.

"They must be very good artists," observed Margo. "His coat of fur looks real."

Derek gasped. "It *is* real! It's moving."

"He hasn't seen us," whispered Margo. "Quick, behind this rock and be very still."

Derek peeked out. "He's going toward those lambs."

"But he'll be coming right by us," Moki gulped. "Whatever you do, don't baa-aa."

"He's sure to smell us," breathed Margo.

The three friends fell silent and huddled together in anxious suspense, waiting for the lion to appear. The minutes dragged agonizingly, and still the beast did not come into view. They were even daring to hope that he had gone the other way, when there was a thud, a sudden snarl, and then another.

Moki could stand it no longer. He had to take a look. "You are not going to believe this, but there is a kid out there slinging rocks at the lion."

They all peered out just in time to see the boy load his sling and let fly at the lion again. This time the stone hit the lion sharply on the flank. He gave a yelp and ran away.

"Great work!" Derek came from behind the rock. "You saved our lives."

"I've never seen anything like it," added Moki.

"Weren't you afraid of that lion?" asked Margo.

"The deed was not as brave as it might appear," said the youth. "I know that old lion pretty well. He is mostly growl. I've chased him away before when he tried to get one of the lambs."

Just then a cry sounded. "David, David, where are you?"

"Here," shouted the boy, waving. "That's my brother."

He approached. "Who are these strangers?"

"I am Derek, and this is Margo, and Moki."

"Well, as you heard, my name is David, and this is my brother Eliab. Is there trouble at home?"

Eliab bowed to the strangers, "Greetings, shalom." Then to David, "No, no trouble at home, but there is trouble with the king. You have heard how he suffers now from terrible black moods. One such fit of deep despair has taken him. Some of his advisors think he is going mad. Some even say that God is angry with him and is punishing him."

"I know." David spoke in low, sad tones, "Poor King Saul."

"The king's chief counselor has sent for you, David. They have heard at court of your singing and playing, and they hope that your music may soothe the king."

Margo interrupted. "You mean you play and sing as well as chase lions?"

David smiled, "Music is my second weapon. If my sling does not keep the lions away, my singing will."

"He is too modest," put in Eliab. "David is well known in our land for his playing and singing. He also writes many of his songs."

Moki scratched his head. "Hmm, stones and songs, that makes him a real rock musician."

"And pray what is that?" asked Eliab.

"Don't pay any attention to him," laughed Derek.

"Father says you are to take your harp and go at once, David." Eliab handed over the reigns of the donkey cart. "You can take the cart, I will stay with the flock."

"Then I'm off to the king's palace. May I help you on your way, my friends?"

"That would be great, thanks," Derek said as they climbed aboard.

As the cart lumbered along the crude road, David seemed troubled. "I do hope I can help the king. Israel needs him, and he is a good and brave warrior who can help drive the Philistines from our land."

"Philistines!" Moki started. "We've met up with them already, and they are mean all right. We saw them burn one of your villages."

"These are dangerous times. But," David continued, "I should warn you that going into the royal city with me may also be dangerous. In his present state the king may fly into a rage, if I displease him. His anger might be directed at those with me. You are free to leave if you think it best."

"We're staying," said Margo solemnly.

"Speak for yourself," put in Moki. "First it's Philistines, then lions, and now a mad king." They all fell into a thoughtful silence as they rode into the royal city.

David walked slowly, but with firm steps, into the room where the haggard King Saul sat hunched and tense on his throne. The three friends held their breath, watching from behind a heavy drape. The king was obviously a tall, majestic figure. His features were fine and handsome, though the eyes had no light, and his mouth drooped, causing deep lines on either side of his long straight nose. It was as if some dark veil had fallen over this goodly face.

"Take care," whispered the attendant as David made his entrance. "Above all, do not remind the king of the prophecy of Samuel."

"What prophecy?" asked Margo.

"Long ago," he said in low tones, "the prophet Samuel was led in a vision to the town of Bethlehem to anoint David and declare that one day he would be king of Israel. So you see that he could be in great danger if the king recognizes him and remembers."

"Oh, no," Derek and Moki murmured in the same breath.

David began to strum on his harp while moving steadily toward the troubled king, who sat with his scepter resting on his knees. One fist clenched around the golden shaft, and the king raised his arm. But David kept up his steady advance, still playing. He settled on a low cushion close to the king and began to sing softly.

The king let the scepter fall back onto his knees and settled against his chair to listen as David sang, softly and beautifully:

The Lord is my shepherd; I shall not want.

He maketh me to lie down in green pastures.

He leadeth me beside the still waters.

He restoreth my soul. . . .

By the time the young shepherd had finished his song, the king was sleeping. The tension had passed from his face. David kept strumming lightly.

"Good, the king is asleep," said the attendant to Margo. "But his sleep is fitful, and no one can depend on his mood. The young man is still in grave danger."

This tense situation continued, with David being called to play for the king several times each day, and sometimes deep in the night. However, the music worked magic, and the king's mood remained steady.

This was good, for one day a messenger came bringing news that the feared Philistines had entered the land of Judah and were ravaging the countryside. King Saul questioned the soldier closely and then summoned his captains.

"We will head off the Philistines in the Valley of Elah and drive them out of the land. Call all your men. We will march at once."

David approached the king. "May I accompany you, Sire?"

The king looked fondly at the youth. "No, David, my son, battle is not for boys. You must return to your father and tell him that you have found favor in my eyes."

Early next morning David took his harp, the old donkey cart, and with his new friends started back to his father's house in Bethlehem.

The old man, Jesse, welcomed the little company, "Shalom, shalom, friends of my son. Our home is your home. You have come just in time for a meal. We honor your three brothers, David—Eliab, Shammah, and Abinadab—who are going to help the king in his fight against the Philistines."

The newcomers found places at the table and when they had eaten their fill, Jesse

saluted the three young men. "Conduct yourselves bravely, my sons, and may the Lord our God have you in his keeping."

Margo, Moki, and Derek spent a peaceful month in Jesse's home, helping David with his chores and learning the ways of sheep and goats as they tended and drove the herds.

But as the days went by, they could see that old Jesse was worried. No word had come from the battlefront. One morning he summoned David and instructed him to load the cart with provisions and go to seek out his brothers. Of course, Moki, Derek, and Margo would not miss out on this adventure, so they climbed aboard the cart.

"Do you think your army can handle the Philistines, David?" asked Derek as they rode along.

"It won't be easy," he replied. "They are very fierce, and they have many weapons of brass and iron."

"Sounds one-sided to me," said Moki.

"It isn't," David spoke confidently. "We are fighting for our homeland, the land that the Lord our God has given us. He will help us defend it."

"I see tents ahead," cried Margo as they topped the next hill. There in front of them lay the whole Israelite encampment. It looked very quiet and peaceful.

Moki rolled his eyes. "This is going to be like looking for a needle in a haystack."

Actually, it did not take long to find Eliab, Abinadab, and Shammah, for David made inquiries and soon located the camp of the tribe of Judah.

"I bring greetings and gifts from our father. He is worried about you and has sent me to find how the battle is going."

"We are quite well," said Eliab, though his tone was strangely cool.

"How is the battle going?" asked Derek.

There was an awkward pause. At last Abinadab spoke, but he did not answer the question. Rather, he turned attention to the supplies on the wagon. "Look, cheese and bread and . . ."

A booming voice interrupted him. A Philistine was shouting from the sandy hill just across a small stream. When David looked he saw an enormous man towering above the rest of the Philistine army. "Israelites, have you found a man who will meet my challenge? Send him out. I grow lonely here. We can avoid the battle if only you will send one brave man to fight with me. If I kill him, you will be our slaves, and if he kills me"—he paused to laugh—"we will be your slaves. What are you waiting for? Have you no brave men?"

"What does this mean?" asked David. "Has no member of the army of Israel gone out to meet this Philistine?"

Eliab turned on his little brother bitterly, "It is very well for you to ask such a question, but look at that man. He is a giant. Who could possibly defeat such a man? You should be at home with the sheep."

Moki was excited. "That's the giant Goliath we saw back in the Philistine camp. He fought six men at one time and defeated them all."

"I sure wouldn't fight him" said Derek. "I've seen him in action."

"I am growing impatient," the voice roared again. "For forty days I have waited, but I will not wait forever. I return tomorrow to defy the armies of Israel. Send out a man."

A soldier nearby spoke to David. "King Saul has offered the man who defeats Goliath great riches and the hand of his daughter in marriage. Even with so great a reward, no one dares go against this mighty champion."

"The king's daughter would be an

instant widow," Moki commented.

"This is indeed strange," said David. "Goliath of Gath is but a man, and you are soldiers of the living God. Why are you afraid?"

"Hold your tongue, young one," snapped Eliab. "You know nothing of fighting. You have never done anything but tend sheep. Go back to that business and leave the battle to us."

David's words were quiet but determined, "If no one else will fight this Philistine, I will."

The youth's brave words soon reached the ears of the king, who sent for him. "Is it true you are willing to fight this Philistine?"

"Yes, Sire." David bowed to the king.

"You are but a lad. I sent you home, why are you here?"

"I came to bring food to my brothers and heard this disgraceful challenge. It must not go unanswered."

"You are but a boy. What do you know of the ways of war?" The king paused. "What can such a one as you do against this giant? All men fear him."

"I do not." David raised his head. "In the fields I have fought against lions and bears, and God has helped me to conquer such fierce beasts when they came to take our lambs. I will do the same to this Philistine who comes to take our people."

"Your spirit pleases me," said the king, smiling. "But you must have armor. Take my helmet and shield and your choice of my best weapons. May God go with you."

Attendants began to load the pieces of armor onto David until he staggered. "By your leave, Sire, I will not take these. They are too heavy. I cannot move."

"But they will protect you, David."

"I do not need protection other than what our God will

provide. I do not go to defend myself, I go to attack."

The king shook his head. "You cannot attack without a weapon." He unstrapped his jeweled sword.

"I need only my staff and sling. Those were my weapons against the lion and against the bear. God delivered them into my hand." David bowed again to the king and left the tent.

Outside the royal tent everyone was talking about the uneven contest that would take place the next day. David's older brothers were visibly moved.

"I cannot believe he is willing to do this," Eliab muttered.

"He has never been short of courage," said Shammah.

"You can say that again," put in Moki.

"There is something about David," Margo remarked. "He has such faith and courage. Perhaps that is the only way to defeat Goliath."

Abinadab nodded, "Perhaps you are right."

Next day the ranks of the army of Israel lined up on one bank of the stream that ran

through the Valley of Elah. Moki, Derek, and Margo placed themselves where they would have a good view. A heavy silence hung over the scene. The only movement was a small bird flying to perch on the spear Goliath had thrust into the ground.

Suddenly the air rang with the giant's derisive laughter, and the taunting challenge signaled his approach. King Saul moved forward and stood with his hand on David's shoulder as the giant's great bulk came into view. His brawny legs were encased in brass leggings, and he had a heavy plate of brass on his chest. The helmet on his head was so heavy that no other man could wear it. He swaggered across the sand and put his hand upon the shaft of his spear. "Ho, Israelites, I challenge you again. Send someone to fight me. Is no one among you man enough?"

This was too much for Eliab. "We cannot let this happen, brothers. I will go to die in his place."

But it was too late. David was already wading across the stream. At first, Goliath ignored the approaching youth, for it didn't occur to him that this could be his contestant. But as David continued to advance, the expression on the giant's face changed. "What is this? Is a boy the best that the tribes of Israel can send?"

"I am a soldier of the living God, the God of Israel," called David.

"A soldier?" sneered the giant. "You have no weapons." David held out his staff. "Am I a dog that you come against me with a stick?" snarled Goliath.

David let his staff fall to the ground. "I shall defeat you without it." He came steadily on.

At this Goliath began to seethe with rage. "You insolent one, I will carve your flesh and feed it to the fowls of the air and to the wild beasts."

"It is you, Goliath, who will be food for the beasts, so that all will know that the God of Israel is the Lord of the earth."

In his fury, Goliath had drawn his great sword. He held it above his head and waved it at the ranks of Philistines, who gave a loud cheer. Then, swinging the blade in wide swaths, he began striding toward David.

The youth had selected a stone from his pouch and put it into his sling, which he began to swing in a wide, slow circle above his head. His eyes never left the giant, who was getting nearer and nearer.

When Goliath was within a few yards of the boy, he put both huge hands on the handle of his sword and raised it above his head for the death blow.

David stood still, stock still, his sling whirling faster and faster. Then he took a single step forward, snapped his wrist sharply, and sent the stone speeding to its mark. It struck the mighty man, sinking into his forehead.

David dropped to one knee as the giant kept coming. To the watchers on the bank it looked as if the stone had no effect. Only a startled look crossed Goliath's face, nothing more, and he held his sword still over his head. But then, his knees began to buckle. He was staggering but still approaching David, who had not budged from his position, and still brandishing his sword. Then with a huge crash, like an enormous oak uprooted by the wind,

Goliath fell dead, not an arm's length from the crouching boy.

The Israelites stood in stunned silence. As they began to realize what had happened, they broke into a ringing cheer, and started in hot pursuit of the confused Philistines. David's brothers paused long enough to slap the young hero on the back. But David knelt beside the fallen giant quietly praying.

King Saul stood beside the lad who had saved Israel from the Philistines. The king could see that the Lord God was with David and that all his undertakings would be blessed with success, and King Saul stood in awe of him.

As Derek, Moki, and Margo looked on, something of the meaning of what had happened came clear to them. "Do you realize that David is the one who will become the great King David?" asked Margo.

"Yes," said Derek, "I do, and I'll never forget him."

"I sure wish I hadn't covered my eyes for most of the fight," sighed Moki. "I missed the best part."

"The best is yet to come." Derek beckoned to his friends. "We have a long way to go. We'd better be on our way."

They turned and started down the hill.